I L@ve you missca

You are the#1 Best

BODY TALK

THE PULSE OF LIFE

THE CIRCULATORY SYSTEM

JENNY BRYAN

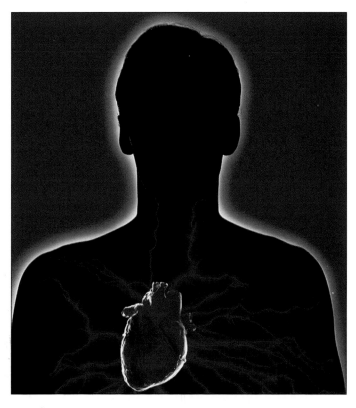

Dillon Press
New York

BODY TALK

BREATHING

REPRODUCTION

DIGESTION

MIND AND MATTER

MOVEMENT

SOUND AND VISION

SMELL, TASTE AND TOUCH

THE PULSE OF LIFE

Cover and title page: Special effects photograph showing the position of the heart.
Editor: Catherine Baxter
Series Design: Loraine Hayes
Consultant: Dr. Tony Smith—Associate Editor of the *British Medical Journal*

First Dillon Press edition 1993

Dillon Press
Macmillan Publishing Company
866 Third Avenue
New York, NY 10022

Macmillan Publishing Company is part of the Maxwell Communication Group of Companies.

First published in 1992 by Wayland (Publishers) Limited
61 Western Road, Hove, East Sussex, England BN3 1JD

Library of Congress Cataloging-in-Publication Data

Bryan, Jenny
   The pulse of life : the circulatory system / Jenny Bryan.
      p.   cm. — (Body talk)
   Includes bibliographical references and index.
   Summary: Discusses the circulatory system, with an emphasis on the heart, its diseases, and ways of staying healthy.
   ISBN 0–87518–566–5
   1. Cardiovascular system—Juvenile literature. [1. Circulatory system. 2. Heart.]   I. Title. II. Series.
QP103.B78 1993
612.1—dc20   92-36410

Printed by G. Canale C.S.p.A., Turin, Italy

10 9 8 7 6 5 4 3 2 1

CONTENTS

INTRODUCTION

Your heart is your most important organ. It keeps you alive. You can manage with one lung, one kidney, and only a small part of your liver. But when the heart stops beating, the rest of the body dies almost immediately.

The body is made up of billions of cells and these need the oxygen and food that are carried in the blood. If the heart stops pumping blood around the body through arteries and veins, the cells die.

It was the ancient Egyptians who discovered that we have a heart. They had to take it and other organs out of dead bodies before they could preserve them as mummies. But Hippocrates—the Greek doctor whose writings still influence the way doctors work—believed that the arteries contained air. It was another 2,000 years (1628) before the British doctor William Harvey showed that the heart pumps blood around the body in a circle. The blood goes out of the heart in vessels (tubes) called arteries and comes back in vessels called veins. This is known as circulation.

We should all take great care of our hearts. Unfortunately, few of us do. In industrialized countries such as Britain, the United States, and Australia, more people die from heart disease than from anything else. The number of British people who die every day from heart disease could fill a jumbo jet! Smoking, an unhealthy diet, high blood pressure, lack of exercise, and being overweight are just a few of the hazards of twentieth century living that lead to heart disease.

No one lives forever. But by looking after our hearts from an early age we can lead more healthy, active, and happy lives.

LEFT According to ancient Egyptian legend, Anubis, "the Lord of the Mummy Wrapping," pictured here with the jackal's head, was in charge of the ceremony in which the heart of a dead person was weighed in preparation for entering the underworld. If the heart didn't weigh the right amount, the dead person wasn't allowed in and was eaten up instead.

OPPOSITE Getting plenty of exercise when you are young strengthens your heart. It can also be great fun!

IN THE WOMB

The heart is the first organ that forms in an embryo. It can be seen beating in the sixth week of pregnancy when the unborn child is smaller than a baked bean and doesn't even look like a human being. By twelve weeks the heart can pump blood around the body.

While the fetus is in the womb, it relies on its mother's blood for oxygen and food and for getting rid of waste products. Blood passes between mother and child through the umbilical cord.

Blood that is rich in oxygen and nutrients goes to the fetal heart. This heart pumps the blood to the brain and other organs, much as it does after birth. But when the blood needs more oxygen, it goes back to the mother instead of going to the lungs of the fetus. This happens all the time that the baby is in the womb. As it gets larger, the fetus needs more and more oxygen and nutrients.

When it is born, the baby must quickly adapt to life outside the womb. The blood supply from its mother stops at the moment of birth. The newborn baby's blood must now get its oxygen by passing through the baby's own lungs. It is vital the baby starts to breathe so that there is oxygen in its lungs for the blood to collect.

After the baby's first feeding, nutrients pass from its intestines into its blood and these are also carried around the body.

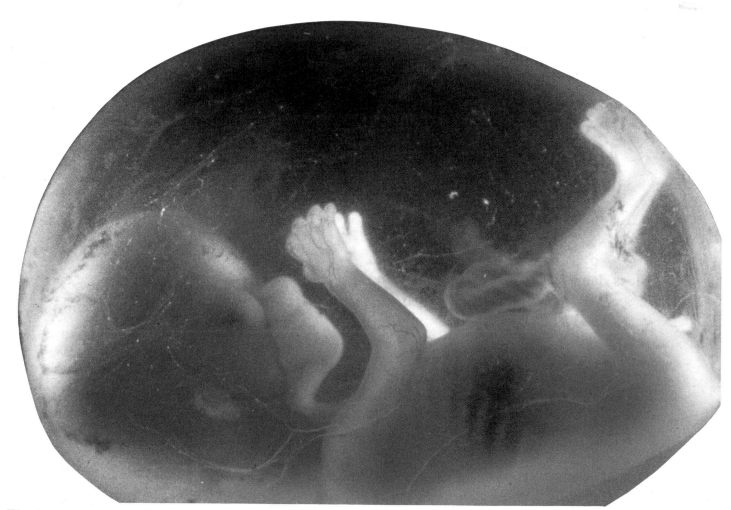

The human fetus at fourteen weeks. Its heart can already pump blood around its body.

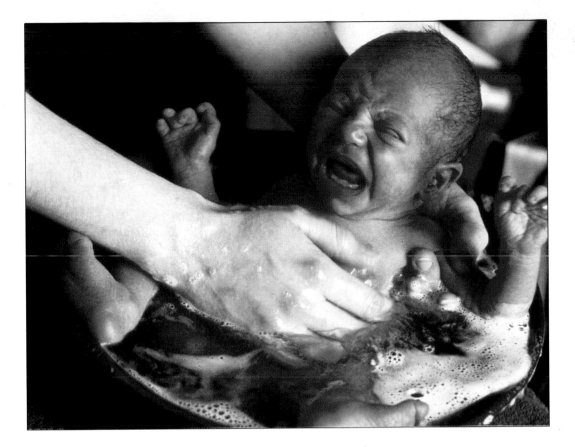

Minutes after being born, this baby girl adapted to life outside the womb. She could no longer rely on her mother's blood for oxygen and nutrients and had to get them for herself.

WHAT CAN GO WRONG

Some babies are born with abnormal hearts. This can mean parts of the heart are missing or the arteries and veins to the heart may be joined incorrectly. The most common problem is a hole in the heart. This happens when the passage that allows blood to bypass the lungs before birth fails to close. It is dangerous because eventually the lungs become badly damaged.

Babies who look blue may not have enough oxygen going around their bodies and may need an emergency operation to correct their heart defect. Doctors can now discover many of these so-called congenital heart problems while the baby is still in the womb. They can use sound waves to produce pictures on a TV screen of the insides of a baby's body. If they discover there is something wrong with the baby's heart or another of its organs, they can prepare to operate soon after it is born. Some babies have even had operations when they were still in the mothers' womb. But this is still relatively rare and normally surgeons don't operate until the baby has been born.

By operating earlier than they used to, doctors can now help babies born with even some of the most serious heart problems to grow up healthy. Ten or more years ago, such babies would have died at a very young age.

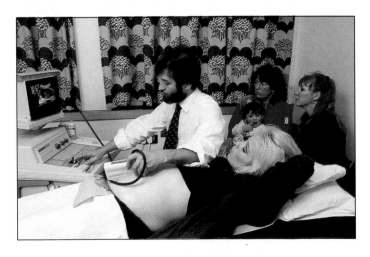

During pregnancy doctors can scan the womb to check the baby's development.

HOW YOUR HEART WORKS

Your heart is in the middle of your chest, between your lungs. A woman's heart weighs about 5.5 pounds while a man's weighs about 6.6 pounds. Each day it pumps about 24,000 quarts of blood around the body, enough during a lifetime to fill a buildin the size of New York City's Empire State Building.

The heart is a muscular pump made up of four parts—the left atrium and the right atrium at the top and the left and right ventricles at the bottom. Blood vessels from the lungs carry blood rich in oxygen into the left atrium. From there it passes down through a valve into the left ventricle. This pumps blood out into the aorta—a big artery that carries blood around the body. Smaller arteries off the aorta take the blood to all the other organs and tissues, where oxygen and nutrients are taken out to feed the cells.

The used blood is then carried back to the right side of the heart by veins. It passes into the right atrium and down into the right ventricle. From there it is pumped to the lungs to collect more oxygen and the cycle continues.

The speed at which the heart beats is controlled by many nerves. These carry electrical signals to the heart muscle. When you are very active—for example, when you are running fast or climbing a steep flight of stairs—your heart will need to pump faster so that more oxygen gets around your body. When you are asleep, your heart beats more slowly because you need less oxygen.

Like any other organ, the heart needs a blood supply to give it oxygen and nutrients. The heart gets its blood supply from the coronary arteries that lead off the aorta.

Heart transplant pioneer Christiaan Barnard

HEART TRANSPLANTS

The first heart transplant was performed in 1967 by the surgeon Christiaan Barnard. The patient lived less than two weeks. Nowadays, heart transplants are done routinely all over the world. In many places, at least three-quarters of patients live five or more years after their transplant and lead near-normal lives.

This success is due to the skill of the surgeons and to better drugs to prevent patients' bodies from rejecting new hearts. But there is still a shortage of hearts. Too few people carry donor cards and some doctors do not like to ask grieving relatives for the organs of someone who is dying.

A few people have been given artificial hearts, but these are unlikely ever to work as well as the real thing. Scientists are also testing muscle grafts. Pieces of muscle are wrapped around a sick heart to help it pump blood around the body.

A   Oxygenated blood (pink) from the lungs enters the left atrium.
     Deoxygenated blood (blue) enters the right atrium.
B   Blood is forced through the valves into the ventricles.
C   As the ventricles begin to contract, the valves close.
D   Blood is pumped to the lungs to collect more oxygen.

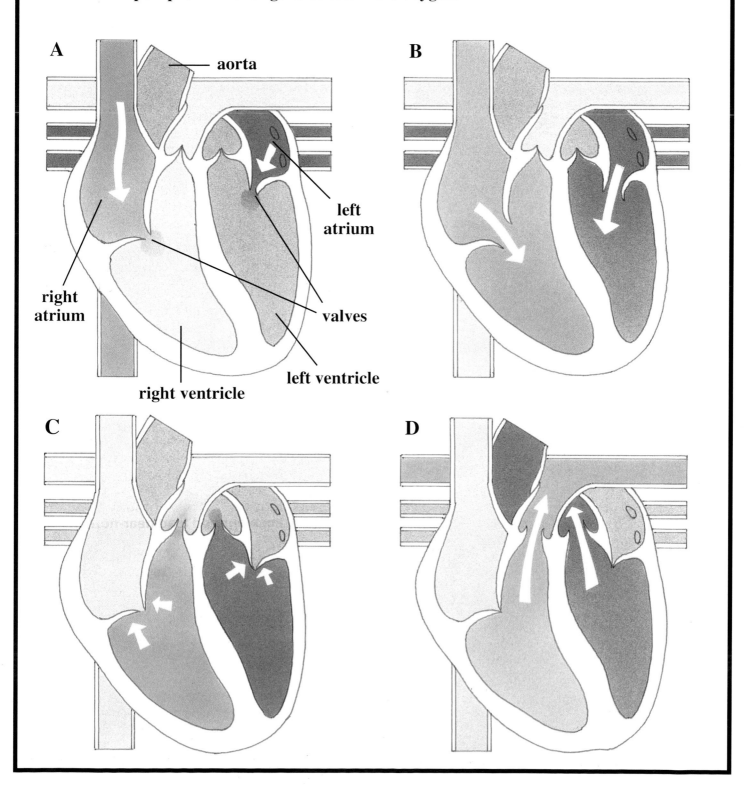

TAKING YOUR PULSE

One of the first things a doctor will do when you feel ill is take your pulse. It shows how fast your heart is beating.

The heart normally beats around seventy times a minute. But it beats much faster in babies and more slowly in elderly people.

Your heart will beat faster when you are running around, if you are worried or frightened, or if you have a high temperature. It slows down when you are asleep or relaxed or if you are very fit.

You can feel your pulse most easily in arteries that are near the surface of your skin—for example, in your wrist, your ankle, or your neck. At these places you may even be able to see your pulse moving.

To take your pulse, place two fingers of your right hand over the inside of your left wrist, a little over halfway across (or ask someone to help you). If you are left-handed, you may find it easier to take the pulse in your other wrist. Never use your thumb to take your pulse, as this will make it harder to take correctly.

You should feel a regular movement in your wrist. This is your blood passing through your arteries in time with your heartbeat. Use a stopwatch or the second hand of your watch to count how many times your heart beats in a minute.

To see how fit you are, take your pulse before and after doing some exercise. If you run hard for fifteen or twenty minutes, your pulse will go up. The more fit you are, the harder you will have to run to make it increase. A fit person's pulse will return to normal more quickly when he or she stops running than the pulse of someone who is unfit.

When you take someone's pulse, be sure to place your fingers on that person's wrist. If you use your thumb, you will get a double reading or "echo" caused by the movement of blood through the thumb itself.

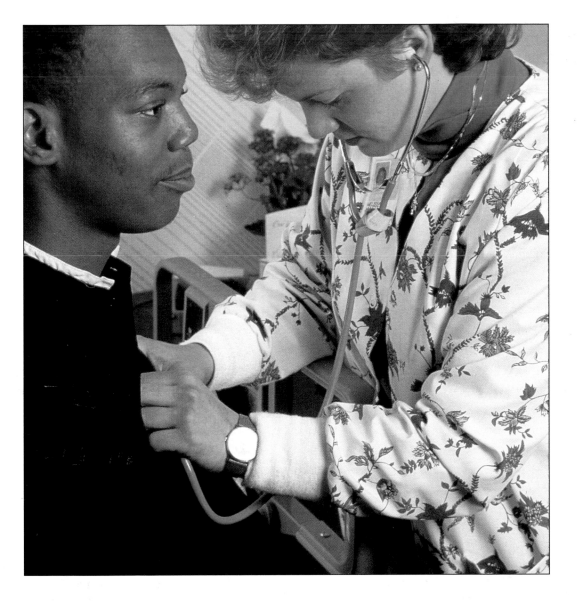

A nurse listens to a patient's heartbeat through a stethoscope. She wants to hear a strong, regular sound. If she thinks there's something wrong, she'll send him for more detailed tests.

BELOW A young woman has biofeedback to help her relax.

BIOFEEDBACK

You can learn to lower your pulse by willing it to go down! This is a useful way to help you relax. It is called biofeedback. Ideally, you should be linked to a machine that takes your pulse continuously and tells you what it is. But these machines are expensive. You can try biofeedback by getting someone else to take your pulse and tell you what it is, say, every three minutes. Lie down and let your arms and legs go limp. Breathe slowly and deeply. Imagine your heart is beating more and more slowly. Or pretend you are doing something that you find very relaxing.

If you are patient and really relaxed, your pulse will fall. Once you have found out how to reduce your heart rate, you can use this

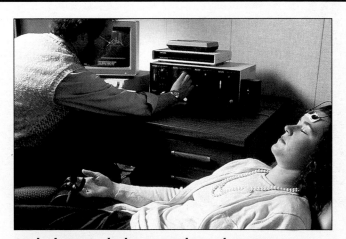

technique to help you relax when you are anxious—for example, before exams or an important sports event.

HEART RHYTHMS

Electrical changes occur in the heart muscle with every single beat. These can be measured by small disks, called electrodes, that are put on the patient's chest.

The pattern of electrical changes that is recorded is called the electrocardiogram, or EKG for short. Everyone's EKG should be roughly the same. Any changes in the pattern may tell the doctor that something is wrong with the heart. An EKG test is very useful and does not hurt at all. Many Doctors can do them in the their offices without even sending you to the hospital.

You may have heard someone complain of having palpitations. They can feel their heart "thumping"—beating fast or unevenly. They may just have run fast or they may be anxious. Cigarettes and strong coffee can also make the heart beat very fast. However, people who often feel that their hearts are racing when there is no obvious reason should see a doctor as soon as possible. An EKG may show that something is wrong and needs treatment. Someone who has had a heart attack, for example, will have a very abnormal EKG and need to be watched carefully for several days afterward to make sure that the EKG returns to normal.

Some people need drugs to control their heartbeat and give them a normal EKG. These drugs work very well and help people with even seriously abnormal heart rhythms to lead normal lives. Without the drugs they would feel tired and ill and they might have a heart attack.

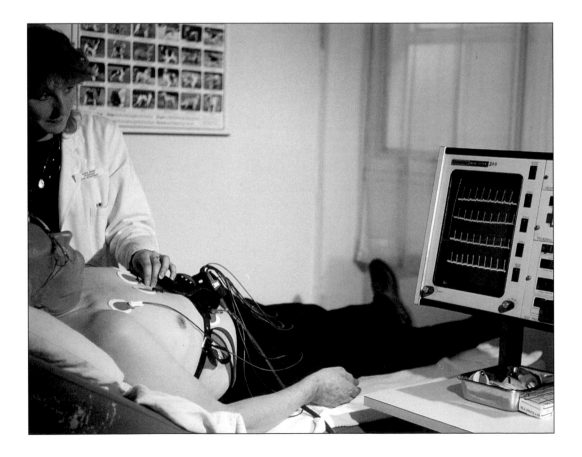

A man with an abnormal heartbeat is wired up to an electrocardiogram (EKG) to find out what is wrong. Some abnormalities do not matter, while others need urgent treatment.

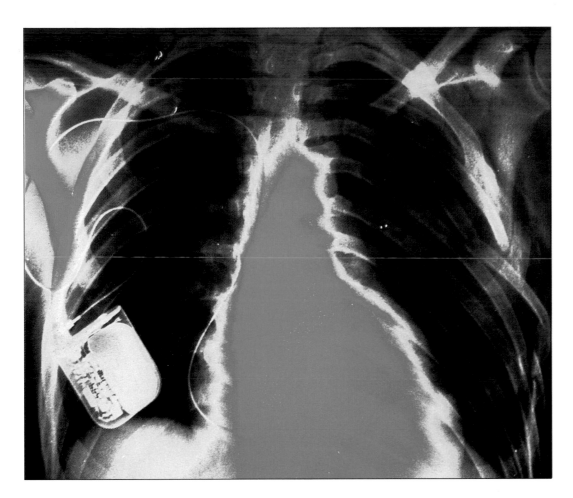

A pacemaker sits comfortably under this patient's skin and she is hardly aware that it is there. Color has been added to the X ray of her chest so that the pacemaker stands out more clearly. The heart lies slightly right of center where the blue color bulges into the outline of the ribcage.

PACEMAKERS

Sometimes it is not possible to correct an abnormal heart rhythm with drugs. Some people need a device called a pacemaker to be put in under their skin. This sends out electrical signals to make their hearts beat properly.

A modern pacemaker

The first pacemaker was used in 1957. It weighed over a pound and lasted just a few months. Today's pacemakers weigh less than an ounce and last up to ten years. A pacemaker makes the heart muscle contract at the right speed. It can even make it speed up or slow down depending on whether the person is resting or active.

It takes just half an hour and a local anesthetic for a physician to insert a pacemaker. The control box lies below the collar bone or under the breast, and wires poke down into the blood vessels into the heart. These make the heart muscle contract so that blood is pumped through the body.

Most people who need pacemakers are in their sixties and seventies. And more women have them than men, although this is probably because women live longer. The heart may have been damaged by a heart attack or heart disease, or it may simply have worn out—seventy years is a long time! A slow heart rate is the most likely reason for putting in a pacemaker.

TAKING YOUR BLOOD PRESSURE

Measuring your pulse or having an EKG are not the only ways of finding out if your heart and circulation are working well. The pressure at which your blood goes through your arteries is also very important. If it is too high, it may damage your heart, brain, and other organs. But if it is too low, you will faint.

If your doctor measures your blood pressure, he or she will take two readings: the first when your heart is beating and the second when it is resting between beats. The first reading is called the systolic blood pressure. This is always considerably higher than the second reading, which is called the diastolic blood pressure.

This little girl is listening to her blood pulsing through her arteries. The gauge on the cuff around her arm will tell the doctor what her blood pressure is. Blood pressure increases with age. So this child's pressure will probably be less than her doctor's.

To take your blood pressure your doctor will first wrap a piece of material around your arm above your elbow and inflate it. This cuff has to be quite tight to stop the blood flow in your arm. It may feel uncomfortable, but it does not hurt.

The cuff is slowly deflated and the doctor listens to the pulse in your elbow through a stethoscope. When the doctor first hears blood coming through the arteries, he or she reads the pressure gauge attached to the cuff. This shows the pressure that the cuff is still putting on your arm. Since your blood is able to get through your arteries despite the cuff, it must be at the same pressure as the cuff. This is the systolic pressure.

As the cuff deflates more, the doctor can hear the blood start to flow smoothly and regularly through your arteries. The pressure at which this happens is the diastolic pressure.

Both blood pressure readings are taken in millimeters of mercury—mm Hg, for short. A healthy young adult has readings of 110/75 mm Hg. These rise to about 130/90 mm Hg by the age of sixty.

If blood pressure is too high, it can cause strokes and heart attacks.

TREATING HIGH BLOOD PRESSURE

Nearly one in three adults in the United States have blood pressure that is too high. They need treatment to bring their blood pressure down to normal levels. Sometimes this can be done by changing what people eat and how they live. Alcohol, being overweight, eating too much salt, and getting too little exercise can all lead to high blood pressure. So people should get rid of these problems first.

If the person's blood pressure still stays too high, he or she can take drugs to reduce the pressure. Most of these make the arteries wider. This means there is more room for the blood to get through and so the pressure falls. Some people need two, three, or even more drugs to control their blood pressure. Although in the past little was known about how to treat high blood pressure, today nearly everyone can be cured. However, it is better to live healthily and avoid the problem in the first place.

You can help to avoid high blood pressure and heart disease by following these simple rules: Eat healthy foods, keep away from fatty food, exercise, don't smoke, and learn to relax.

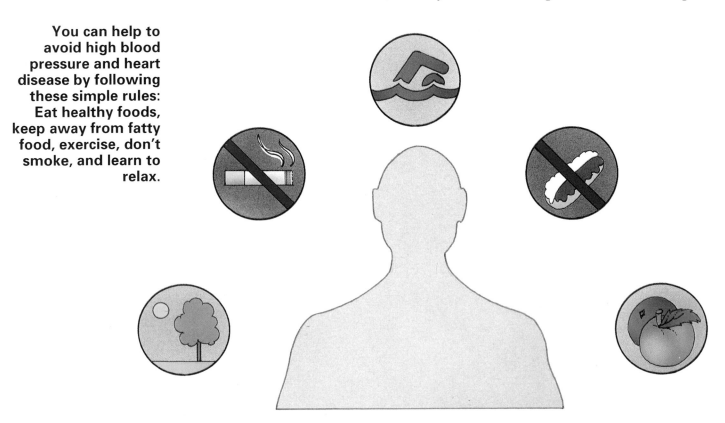

BLOOD

Blood is the life force of the human body. It moves around your body twenty-four hours a day, every day of your life. It acts as a conveyor belt, a gas supply, a waste disposal unit, a first-aid kit, an early warning system, and a defense force.

Blood consists of billions of cells that float in a liquid called plasma. There are three main groups of cells: red cells, white cells, and platelets.

Red cells give blood its striking color. They are red because they contain a pigment called hemoglobin. It is hemoglobin that carries life-giving oxygen from the lungs to every single living cell in the body.

There are several different types of white cells. Their job is to protect the body from invaders such as bacteria and viruses and to fight infection.

Platelets are the first-aid kings. If you cut yourself and start to bleed, your platelets will rush to the injury and stick together to plug the wound and start to form a scab.

Blood also acts as a general transportation system. Nutrients from your food get to cells in the blood and waste products are carried away from cells to your kidneys ready to be excreted. If you take a medicine such as aspirin for a headache, your blood carries it to the place where it is needed.

These are the three main types of cells in your blood—red cells, white cells and platelets.

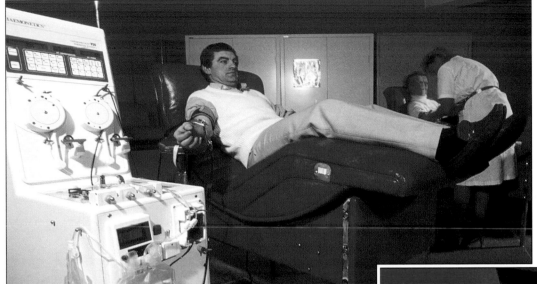

There's nothing frightening about giving blood. This man will probably get a drink and a cookie afterward, too! And he knows that he may be saving someone else's life with his donation.

BLOOD GROUPS

On the surface of your red cells are proteins that act as "fingerprints" for your blood. There are two main types of protein.

Human blood falls into one of four main blood groups. People with blood group A have one type of protein on their red cells. People with blood group B have the other. People with blood group AB have both types of protein on their red cells.

People with blood group O have neither type. Group O is the most common blood group in both white and black people in the United States. But group A is much more common in whites than blacks. Group B is more common in blacks than whites.

There is another important type of blood grouping, called Rhesus. Eight out of ten people have a protein in their red cells which is the same as that in Rhesus monkey blood. They are Rhesus, or Rh, positive. Those who do not have the protein are said to be Rhesus, or Rh, negative.

Many people go to special clinics to give blood. This is stored for use in transfusions.

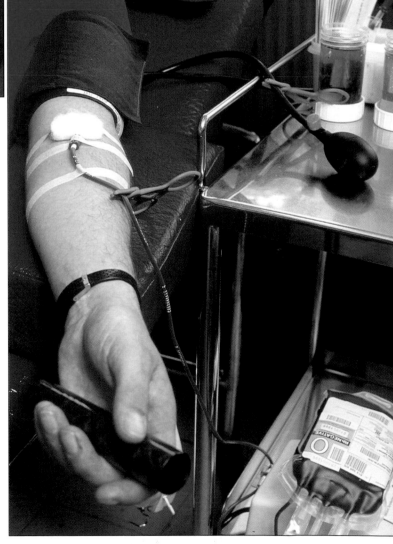

This man has a rare blood group—Rh negative. So his donation at the clinic is very important.

BLOOD TRANSFUSIONS

It is useful to know your blood group in case you ever need a blood transfusion. This is because it is dangerous to be given blood of a group different than your own.

Each year millions of people are given blood transfusions. If you lose a lot of blood—for example, in an accident or during an operation—your body simply cannot replace it quickly enough. Without a transfusion you would die.

The first serious attempt at a blood transfusion was made in the seventeenth century when a French doctor gave lambs' blood to a boy. Surprisingly, the boy survived!

It wasn't until 1901, when blood groups were discovered, that it became safe to have blood transfusions. Before then people were unknowingly given blood of the wrong group and died as a result.

If you were given blood of a group different from your own body's, you would know immediately that the blood was different. Your blood contains millions of defense proteins called antibodies. These would rush out and attack the strange blood cells, making them clump together. Your white cells would then join the battle, and before long you would have lumps of damaged blood cells thudding through your arteries.

If a transfusion of the wrong type of human blood can cause this much damage, imagine what would happen if you were given blood from another animal, such as a dog or a horse, which is even more alien to us.

Unfortunately, there are often shortages of donated blood for transfusion. Donated blood only keeps for about a month and then it has to be thrown away. For many years, scientists have tried to make blood in the laboratory but with little success. One advance that has been made, however, is that it is now possible to save blood lost during operations, clean it, and give it back to its owner later on. This reduces the amount of donated blood that is needed.

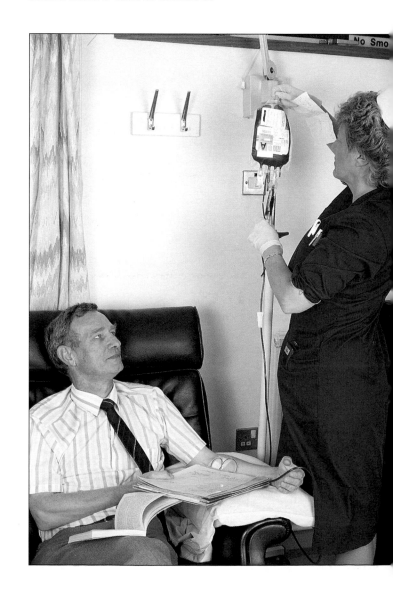

A nurse arranges a blood transfusion for this patient. Although he has to keep very still while the transfusion is in progress, he does not feel any discomfort or pain.

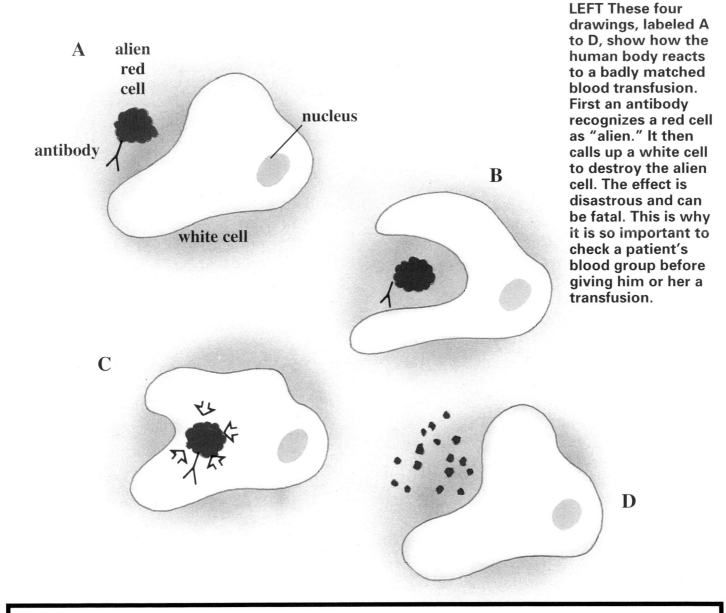

A

alien red cell

antibody

nucleus

white cell

B

C

D

INFECTED BLOOD

In most countries donated blood is tested (right) in case it comes from someone who has AIDS or hepatitis. Both diseases are caused by viruses and can be fatal. People with AIDS are unable to fight infection, and hepatitis is a severe liver disease.

The viruses that cause these diseases are carried in blood. So if someone is given a blood transfusion that contains the virus that causes AIDS or hepatitis that person, too, may get the disease. By testing donated blood for signs of AIDS or hepatitis and removing blood that is infected, doctors can be almost certain that the blood they give to their patients is safe.

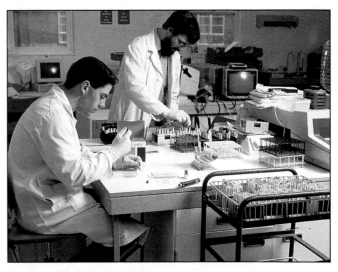

TRAINING FOR A MORE FIT HEART

You, too, could have the heart of an Olympic athlete! But you'll have to train very hard!

Top athletes have bigger hearts than other people. They are up to 25 percent larger! The athletes weren't born with bigger hearts, but by training day after day, the muscles become bigger and stronger. The bigger the heart, the more blood that can be pumped to the arms and legs when racing or playing sports. Sports that use all four limbs, such as swimming, climbing, rowing, and cycling, are best for the heart.

To make your heart more fit, you will need to make it work harder and more efficiently. When you are sitting down, your heart will beat around seventy times per minute. But when you are running around or playing sports, it can go up to 200 or more.

If you want to get fit, you will need to increase your maximum heart rate. You can work out what this should be by subtracting your age from 220.

ABOVE Long-distance runner Liz McColgan (right) demonstrates the physical and mental strength that have taken her to the top.

LEFT German swimmer Kristin Otto, winner of six Olympic gold medals

American swimmer Matt Biondi. Swimming is one of the best sports for training your heart.

If you are eleven years old, you should try to increase your pulse to about 209 beats per minute. You won't be able to keep that up for long! After a few minutes, reduce your exercise level to about three-quarters of your maximum. If you are eleven years old, that will be about 157. Try to keep it there for at least twenty minutes.

Getting fit takes time and you should build up your fitness slowly. As you become more fit, you will find that you have to train harder to make your pulse rate go up. Athletes have resting heart rates as low as forty or fifty, going down to twenty-five or thirty when they are asleep!

Your heart rate will also return to normal more quickly when you stop exercising. It should take as little as two minutes for your heart rate to come down from 157 to 100 and a little longer for it to return to normal. These are good signs! They mean that you are well on your way to your first Olympic gold medal!

MUSCLES

The muscle in your heart is different from that in your arms and legs. It is called cardiac muscle and you use it all the time—even when you are asleep. The muscle in your limbs is called skeletal muscle. You don't use it all the time.

There is a third type of muscle in your body, called smooth muscle. This is found in parts of your body that go on working even without you thinking about them. These include your intestines and your blood vessels.

Smooth muscle is simpler than skeletal muscle and it moves more slowly. But it can contract for longer periods of time. Cardiac muscle contracts quite quickly, but like smooth muscle it does not get tired easily. What makes cardiac muscle different from smooth and skeletal muscle is that it beats without any nerve impulses.

FIGHT OR FLIGHT

Have you ever been really frightened? Did you run away? You probably found that you could run much faster than you thought you could. What gave you that extra spurt was a chemical in your body called adrenaline.

Adrenaline is a hormone. Hormones are messengers. They make things happen all over the body. Adrenaline makes the heart beat faster. It also helps to make blood go from one part of the body to another. If you are frightened and want to run away, it will send extra blood to your legs so that you will be able to run faster.

Adrenaline works at other times, too. It's always there for those big moments: when you have to make a speech or say your lines in the school play; when you go in to an exam; when you're being told off; when you're having an argument. You will know when adrenaline is around—you'll feel your heart thumping.

We all need adrenaline to get us through difficult times. But too much worry can be harmful. Few of us like it if our hearts feel like hammers in our chests all the time. Our hearts may be able to stand the pace, but our minds won't.

RIGHT This fight is just for fun! But if it were for real, the adrenaline would be flowing and these children's hearts would be racing.

OPPOSITE PAGE The dealing room of a stockbroker's office must be one of the most stressful places to work. Unless they can deal with the stress, many of these people will be heading for heart attacks.

COPING WITH STRESS

Stress is the word often used to describe the worry we feel when things are getting on top of us: too much work and not enough time to do it.

Some people seem to cope with stress better than others. In fact, some people love it! They are usually people with a "Type A" personality. They are very outgoing, they talk a lot, and they like to be busy all the time. They often try to do several things at once. Some even leave things until the last minute to put more pressure on themselves. "Type B" people do not like so much stress. They aren't so outgoing and they talk less. They tend to do one thing at a time and they like to relax and not to be under pressure all the time.

Some doctors believe that Type A people are more likely to have heart attacks because the stress they appear to thrive on puts too much strain on their hearts. Type B people are usually calmer so their hearts don't have to work as hard.

HEART DISEASE

Heart disease kills more people in industrialized countries than anything else. Approximately 950,000 people in the United States die every year because of heart disease.

Some countries have done better than others in reducing the number of people who die from heart disease. For example, in the United States deaths from heart disease fell by 50 percent between 1970 and 1985. In Australia, Israel, and Canada about 40 percent fewer people died. But in England and Wales the death rate fell by only 11 percent.

Heart disease is not just a major killer. It leaves thousands of people unable to lead normal lives. They cannot work or play sports. They tire easily and get out of breath. They need drugs, some of which have bad side effects. Some people with heart disease need big operations and may take weeks or even months to recover afterward.

The only way to stop all this suffering is to prevent the heart from becoming damaged in the first place. Heart disease occurs when the arteries that carry blood to the heart—to give it oxygen

The comedian Benny Hill is just one of the many thousands of people to have died from a heart attack.

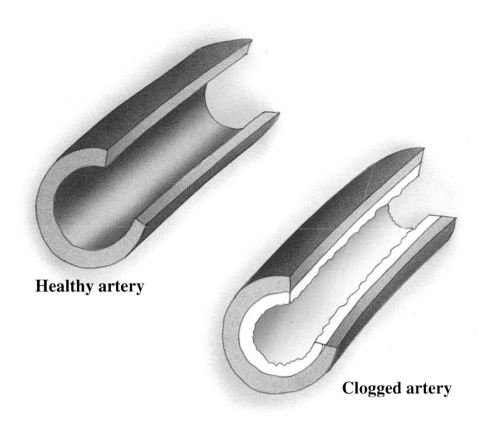

Healthy artery

Clogged artery

and nutrients—become blocked. These arteries are called the coronary arteries.

We are born with healthy arteries. The inner surfaces are smooth, strong, and elastic. This allows them to become wider or narrower according to how much blood must pass through.

As we get older, the arteries can get clogged and become blocked. Fat from the blood gets stuck on the walls of the arteries. The body tries to repair them, but they become scarred. The arteries lose their elasticity and become narrower.

Blood cells start to stick to the uneven walls of the arteries and form clots instead of floating by. Gradually the arteries become blocked and eventually very little blood can get through. Cells nearby that rely on the blood for oxygen and food start to die.

This can happen in any of the arteries in the body. But if it happens in the coronary arteries, the heart is starved of oxygen and stops working properly. If this is not treated, it can lead to a heart attack.

EARLY WARNINGS

When your arteries first become diseased, you won't feel anything. Most people over forty have some damage, but it can start much earlier, even when you are in your teens and twenties.

As the disease gets worse, people start to get symptoms. They may get pains in their chest and feel tired and out of breath. At first this only happens when they are walking around. But eventually it can happen even when they are sitting still or lying down.

As the arteries get narrower, the blood pressure rises. This can be measured by a doctor. Some people take note of these warnings and try to stop the damage from getting worse by eating healthy food and getting more exercise. But this isn't easy. The only way to prevent heart disease is to avoid the things that cause it throughout your life.

WHO IS AT RISK?

Heart disease is far more common in industrialized countries than in developing countries. Because of this, scientists have looked for differences in the way that people live in places such as Africa, India, and South America compared with Europe, the United States, and Australia.

They have found that people who live in the second group of countries are more likely:

- to smoke
- to be overweight
- to eat a lot of fatty and sweet foods
- to eat few fruits and vegetables
- to eat a lot of salt
- to get little exercise

Doctors believe that it is these things that put us at risk of heart disease.

Luckily, you can change the way you eat and the way you live and so reduce your risk of having a heart attack when you are older. But you'll have to start now! It's more difficult to lose weight when you are older, so try not to eat fatty foods now. Find out what your weight should be for your height and build and try to stick to it.

Smoking kills 434,000 people each year in the United States. It is more likely to cause heart disease than any of the other illnesses associated with it. So don't be tempted to start! It's very hard to give up.

Do you dread gym? Exercise is very good for your heart and circulation. If you don't like football or hockey, why not try to find a sport you do enjoy? Swimming is just as good for you, and so are soccer, aerobics, tennis, or basketball. The list is endless!

If you get plenty of exercise now, you could be saving yourself a lot of grief when you are older.

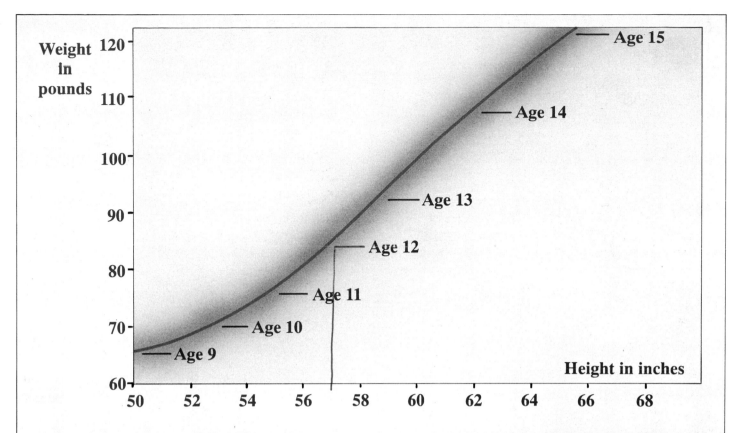

Weight in pounds

120
110
100
90
80
70
60

Age 15

Age 14

Age 13

Age 12

Age 11

Age 10

Age 9

Height in inches

50 52 54 56 58 60 62 64 66 68

Look up your height on this chart and check what your weight should be. Don't worry if you are not exactly on the red line. We are not all identical!

SOME GOOD REASONS TO STOP SMOKING

Smoking doesn't just cause heart disease. It gives you lung cancer, throat cancer, mouth cancer, and many other cancers. It can also give you bronchitis. It makes you cough and wheeze, as well as making your breath smell.

Smoking makes other people ill, too. People who live in smoky homes or work in smoky offices are more likely to get lung disease than those who don't.

Some people who have been smoking for a long time find it very difficult to stop. This is because they have become addicted to the nicotine in tobacco. They may complain of feeling restless and not knowing what to do with their hands.

The best way to avoid these problems is not to start smoking in the first place! Smoking is a very expensive habit, so not only will you look, feel, and smell better, you will also have more money.

"DIET AND HEART DISEASE

What's your favorite food? Do you know what's in it?

It's much easier now than it used to be to find out what's in your food and to see if it's good for your heart. Food packaging often tells you the number of calories in the product and how much fat, protein, and carbohydrate the food contains.

To look after your heart you should cut down on fatty foods, especially those that contain animal fat. Fatty foods are bad for you because the fat is absorbed from your intestine and gets into your blood. Although your body can get rid of some of it, the rest will slowly leak out of your blood and stick to the walls of your arteries.

Foods that are fatty include meat, dairy products, cakes, candy, and cookies. You don't need to give up meat. But lean meats like chicken and fish are better for you than red meats such as pork and beef. Dairy products tend to be very fatty. But you can swap fatty foods like butter and cream for low-fat products such as polyunsaturated margarine and yogurt.

Cooking is important, too. Grilling and baking meat needs less fat than frying. So grilled or roasted meat is better for you than fried meat. Another interesting point is that many fruits and vegetables contain useful vitamins that seem to reduce the damage to your arteries caused by fat.

You don't have to give up junk food completely! You can eat cookies, chips, and chocolate. But try to save them for a treat once or twice a week and not have them every day.

Candy and sugar-filled drinks—just what the doctor didn't order! Food and drink like this should be saved for an occasional snack.

HEARTY EATING

1. Eat broiled or grilled food rather than fried food.

2. If you want to fill up, eat pasta or potatoes
   —not cakes and cookies.

3. When you want something sweet, have a piece of fruit
   —not a chocolate bar.

4. Avoid eating too much cheese, butter, and rich dressings.

5. Give up sugar whenever possible in tea and coffee.

6. Eat lots of vegetables—especially raw ones.

7. Avoid sweet carbonated drinks.

8. Eat white meat like chicken, not red meat like beef.

This chart shows you how to eat well and yet be kind to your heart. Don't worry if you slip up occasionally. As long as you follow it most of the time, you will be doing your heart a favor.

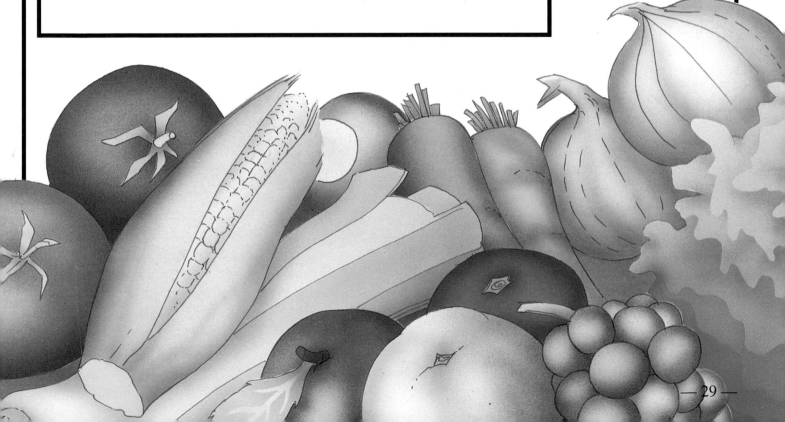

An apple a day keeps the doctor away! Apples contain plenty of healthy fiber and vitamins. They are also much better for your teeth than sugary candies and cookies.

A GOOD START

Children need some fat in their diet to give them energy and help them grow. Some fatty foods also contain nutrients that children need, such as the vitamins and calcium found in milk. In fact, milk is a useful source of many nutrients for children, especially children under five years old, who are not yet eating the same foods as adults. Generally, most children don't need to be as strict with their diet as adults. However, on the whole it is a good idea to avoid foods that contain lots of additives such as artificial colorings and flavorings.

If you get used to eating healthy foods when you are young, you'll find it much easier to stick to a healthy diet when you are older and you'll be less likely to put on weight or be at risk of heart disease. You will also feel better.

SEEING IS BELIEVING

How do doctors know when our arteries are diseased and we need treatment?

You can't listen to an artery to see if it's blocked, and it won't show up on an ordinary X ray. An X-ray picture is made by passing rays through the body. Solid or dense (thick) parts of the body, such as bone, absorb more of the X rays than soft parts. Rays that are not absorbed pass straight through and blacken a photographic plate, which is put behind a patient. If you took an X ray of a blood vessel, you would just get a black smudge. Because a blood vessel is not solid, most of all the rays would pass through.

Cutting someone open to look at his or her arteries is a dangerous step. Doctors have found other ways to look inside our hearts and our arteries.

One way is to inject special dyes into our blood vessels. These dyes show up on X rays. Another way is to bounce extremely high-pitched sound waves off the body. These produce an echo. The type of echo depends on the density of tissue that the sound waves have passed through. These echoes can be turned into a picture on a screen. This second method can be used to watch the blood pulsing through our arteries and our hearts. Any obstacles show up clearly.

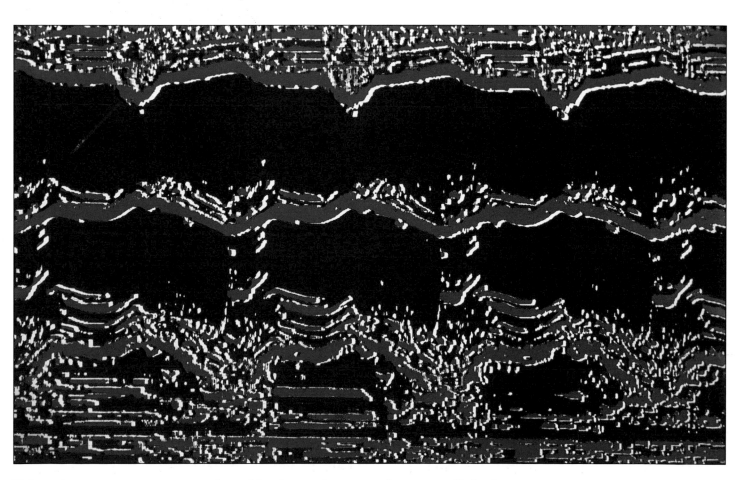

This echosonogram was produced by bouncing sound waves off the heart.

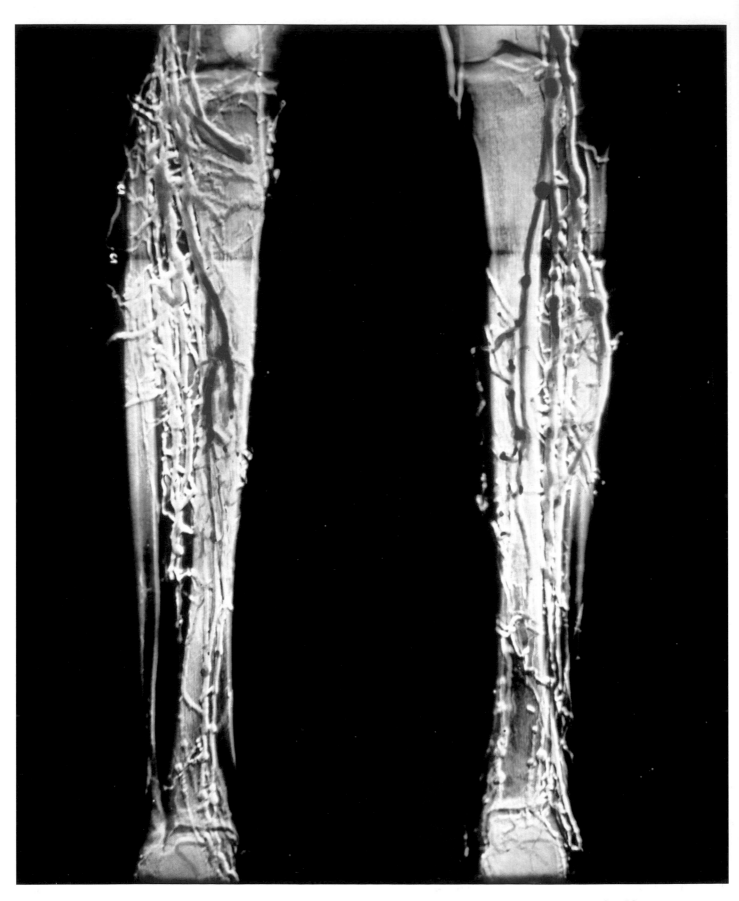

A special dye has been put through this woman's veins so they show up better on the X ray.

UNBLOCKING ARTERIES

As little as twenty years ago, if the arteries to your heart were blocked you would have needed major surgery. A healthy blood vessel would have been taken from your leg and used to bypass the damaged artery and carry blood to your heart. This was a very risky operation indeed and there is a good chance that you would have died.

Now doctors can unblock your arteries without such a major operation. Instead they pass a fine tube into the diseased artery. When it gets to the blockage, the doctors inflate a tiny balloon on the end of the tube. The balloon pushes the plaque that is blocking the artery out of the way so that the blood can flow smoothly again. Some doctors even use lasers to destroy the blockage.

These revolutionary techniques do not cure diseased arteries. In many cases the blockages come back and the treatment has to be done again or the more complicated old-fashioned bypass operation must be done. For some people, however, the new techniques are a lifesaver.

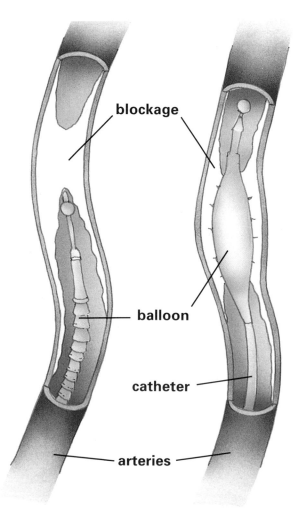

blockage

balloon

catheter

arteries

EMERGENCY

If someone fell down in front of you, clutching his or her chest, would you know what to do? Dial the emergency number and ask for an ambulance. The person could be having a heart attack.

A heart attack occurs when the blood supply to the heart stops. Within minutes cells in the heart start to die. So immediate treatment is vital.

Not all heart attacks are the same. Some may even happen quite slowly. The person complains of feeling unwell for several hours. He or she is very pale and probably has a pain in the chest. But the person may remain conscious throughout. Only an EKG can confirm whether he or she has had a heart attack or not.

A paramedic gives cardiac massage to a man who has suffered a heart attack and whose heart has stopped beating. This sort of first aid is vital to keep people alive until they can be taken to the hospital.

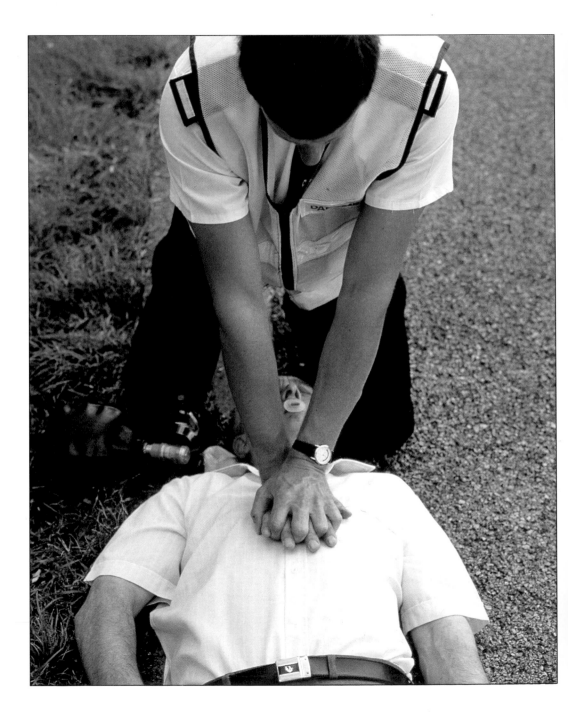

A man who has had a heart attack learns how to look after himself.

Other heart attacks happen much faster and are more severe. Within seconds the person is lying on the floor gasping for breath and losing consciousness. An EKG will reveal a massively abnormal heartbeat.

Both mild and severe heart attacks need immediate hospital treatment. This is because a mild heart attack may be quickly followed by a more severe life-threatening one. When someone has a heart attack, it is important to find out which of the coronary arteries is blocked and to unblock it.

Drugs called anticoagulants should now be given first to dissolve as much of the block as possible before the doctors set to work with their little balloons.

Many major studies have now shown that anticoagulants save lives. Someone who has had a heart attack should also take aspirin, or other drugs that control the way the heart beats, every day for at least a year.

AFTER A HEART ATTACK

Thousands of people lead normal lives after heart attacks. They can go back to work, play sports, and go on trips, just as before. They will, however, need regular checkups. They can help reduce their risk of having another heart attack by keeping at the right weight for their height, by not smoking, by eating a low-fat diet, and by getting plenty of exercise. Many hospitals now run special courses that teach people who have had heart attacks how to get fit and, most importantly, how to stay healthy for the rest of their lives.

A heart attack is often a warning. If people take notice of the warning and look after themselves better, they can live full and active lives.

STROKES

If the blood supply to the brain is suddenly stopped, the cells nearby will die. This is what usually happens when someone has a stroke. When brain cells die other parts of the body may stop working. What happens in the body is similar to what happens during a power outage. All the wires and light bulbs in your home may be working. But if there is no electricity coming from your local power station, none of the things in your home that need electricity will work.

After a stroke a person's arms and legs are still fine, but the nerves in the brain that control how the limbs work may have been damaged. This is why someone who has had a stroke may be paralyzed in the arms or legs, or both. Or his or her face may look twisted because the person can't move part of it anymore. Speech, vision, and even mental ability may also be damaged.

Often the paralysis is on just one side of the body. If, for example, someone has had a stroke in a blood vessel in the left side of the brain, he or she will probably be paralyzed down the right side of the body. This is because of the way the nerves are connected.

Sometimes the nerve cells will recover and the paralyzed arm or leg will start working again. But sometimes the damage is so bad that the paralysis is permanent.

Why does the blood supply to the brain suddenly stop? Like all the other arteries in the body, those leading to the brain can become blocked. Sometimes the strain of the blood trying to get through may make the artery burst. Then blood will rush into all the cells nearby and swamp them.

People with high blood pressure have a greater risk of having strokes than people with normal blood pressure. People who smoke are also at risk of strokes. Strokes are most common in elderly people, but luckily the number of strokes that happen each year is dropping. This is partly because more people are getting treatment for high blood pressure.

The woman on the left has had a stroke in the left side of her brain, leaving her partly paralyzed down her right side and with a speech disorder. The therapist is helping her with her words.

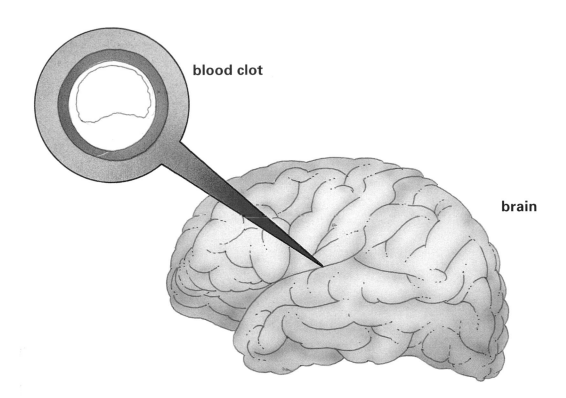

blood clot

brain

SAVING THE BRAIN

Nerves in the brain that are damaged in a stroke release chemicals that spread the damage to other parts of the brain. So scientists are trying to find drugs that will stop this second event. They hope either to prevent the damaged nerves from releasing the dangerous chemicals or to make drugs that will "clean" or neutralize the chemicals before they have a chance to do any more damage in other areas of the brain.

Already they have discovered ways of preventing people who have had one stroke from having another one. A new operation is being done to unblock arteries to the brain so that blood can get through more easily. People can be given aspirin to prevent blood clots from forming and reblocking the arteries to their brain. There is also hope for the future as scientists are at present looking for ways to stimulate damaged nerve cells and make them work again.

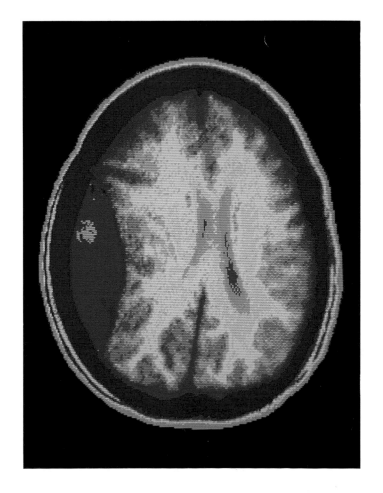

VALVE DISEASE

The valves that lie between the atria and the ventricles of the heart make sure that the blood only goes in one direction. So they are very important. Imagine what would happen if you had blood trying to go in both directions through your arteries and veins at the same time. The result would be complete chaos!

When the left or right atrium at the top of the heart is full of blood, the valve that separates it from the ventricle flips open. This allows blood to pass through and fill the ventricle. Then, when the heart beats, the valve at the other end of the ventricle opens and blood is pumped out into the blood vessels.

From the left side of the heart the blood goes all around the body and from the right side it is carried to the lungs to get some oxygen. The heart valves open and close with the rhythm of the heart. They make sure that blood passes through smoothly and not too fast. Unfortunately, about one in 300 children is born with a faulty valve. The valve opening may be too narrow so blood does not go forward through the heart. Or the valve may be weak and allow blood to flow back up through the heart. Both problems can be dangerous and prevent a child from leading a normal life. But in most cases surgeons can now operate soon after a child is born and correct any faulty valves so that the child can live a normal, healthy life.

Heart valves can also be damaged later in life, either by infection or through normal wear and tear. Rheumatic fever used to be a common cause of valve disease and until the 1960s was almost impossible to do anything about. People who survived rheumatic fever often died some years later from the valve damage that resulted from the sickness.

Because life expectancy is now higher, more people are getting valve problems as a result of normal wear and tear. As we get older, calcium may be deposited on the valves—like in pipes in hard water areas—and stop them from working properly.

NEW VALVES FOR OLD

The first mechanical valve was put into a patient in 1961. Now surgeons routinely replace old or faulty valves with mechanical, animal, or human valves.

Mechanical valves work very much like human ones. As the pressure of blood builds up on one side of the valve, it simply flips open to let the blood through. Then, when enough blood has passed through, the valve flips closed. Ideally, however, surgeons would like to use more human valves, since blood clots are less likely to form on them. But there aren't enough human valves to go around and they do not last nearly as long as the more durable mechanical devices.

Tests are currently being undertaken to improve artificial valves so that they last longer and stay free of blood clots. But it'll be a few more years before they are ready.

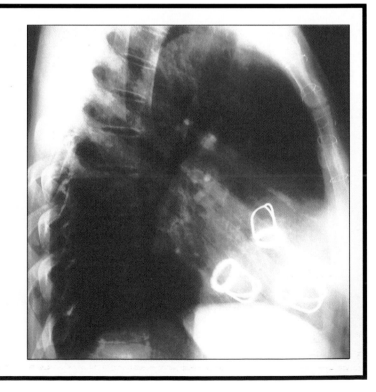

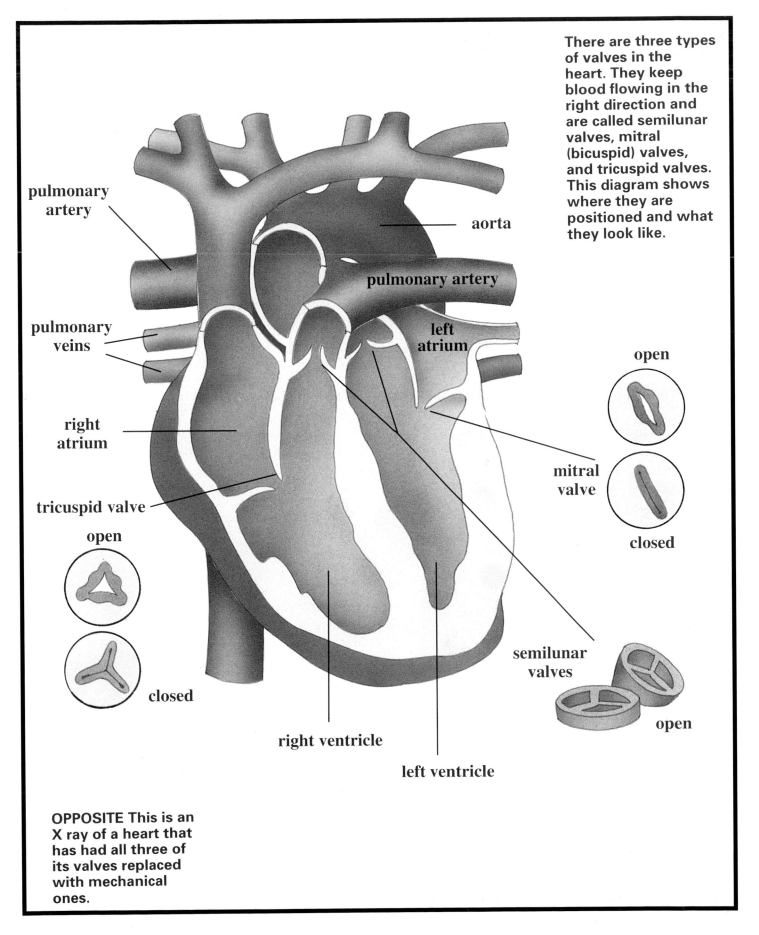

pulmonary artery

aorta

pulmonary artery

pulmonary veins

left atrium

right atrium

tricuspid valve

open

closed

open

closed

mitral valve

open

semilunar valves

right ventricle

left ventricle

There are three types of valves in the heart. They keep blood flowing in the right direction and are called semilunar valves, mitral (bicuspid) valves, and tricuspid valves. This diagram shows where they are positioned and what they look like.

OPPOSITE This is an X ray of a heart that has had all three of its valves replaced with mechanical ones.

VEIN DAMAGE

It isn't only arteries that become diseased as we get older. Veins may also be damaged, and this can be just as dangerous as in arteries.

Most veins have an uphill struggle to get blood back to the heart. For at least sixteen hours a day they are fighting against gravity. Except for when we are lying down, blood must be pumped up from our hands and feet to the central veins in our chest and abdomen. These veins carry the blood to our heart. Our veins contain one-way valves to stop blood from rushing back down our veins when we stand up.

You may know someone who suffers from varicose veins—you can see the veins bulging through the skin of their legs. People who spend a lot of time on their feet or who are overweight are prone to them.

Varicose veins occur when the valves become faulty and blood starts to flow back down the veins. They can occur anywhere in the body but are most common in the legs. They can be very painful, especially when the person who has them walks around. They tend to start in the smaller veins and spread to the bigger, deeper veins. As

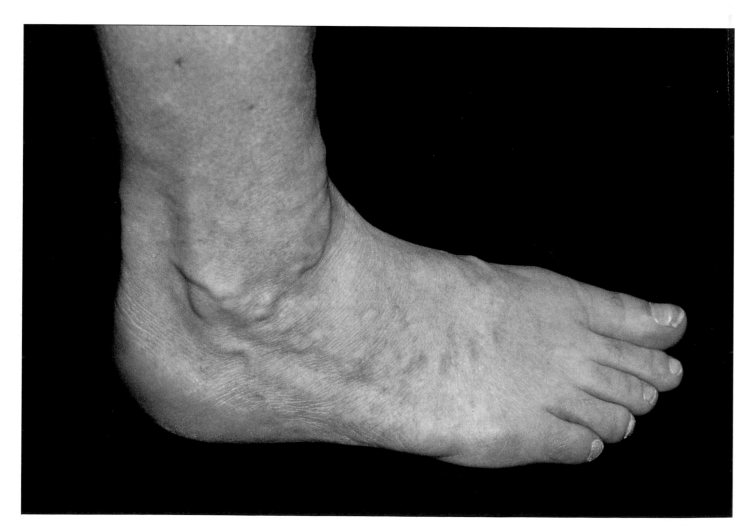

This woman has varicose veins in her ankle. They can be very painful.

pressure builds, the blood supply to the skin may become damaged and some cells may die.

In older people who do not move about very much, ulcers may form on the skin and become infected. These can be very hard to treat. So it is important that anyone with early signs of vein damage, especially if he or she is elderly, should wear support stockings and bandages to improve the blood flow to the skin.

Blood clots are another hazard for veins. They are most common in people who sit or lie down for long periods, allowing their blood flow to slow down and become sluggish.

One reason people are encouraged to get out of bed and move around as soon as possible after an operation is to prevent clots from forming in the deep veins of their legs. If a clot in the leg moves to the brain, heart, or lungs, it can be fatal.

BLOOD CLOTS AND THE PILL

In the 1970s doctors discovered that women who took contraceptive pills were more likely to have strokes, heart attacks, or blood clots forming in their veins than other young women. It soon became clear that it was the hormones in the pill that were responsible. Since then, the amount of hormone put in each tablet has been greatly reduced and the risk of circulatory problems has fallen. The pills shown on the right are the new safer, low-dose variety.

Most women can now safely take the pill without worrying about blood clots. Women who smoke, however, may be advised against taking it, especially if they are over thirty-five and overweight, since smoking also increases the risk of blood clots.

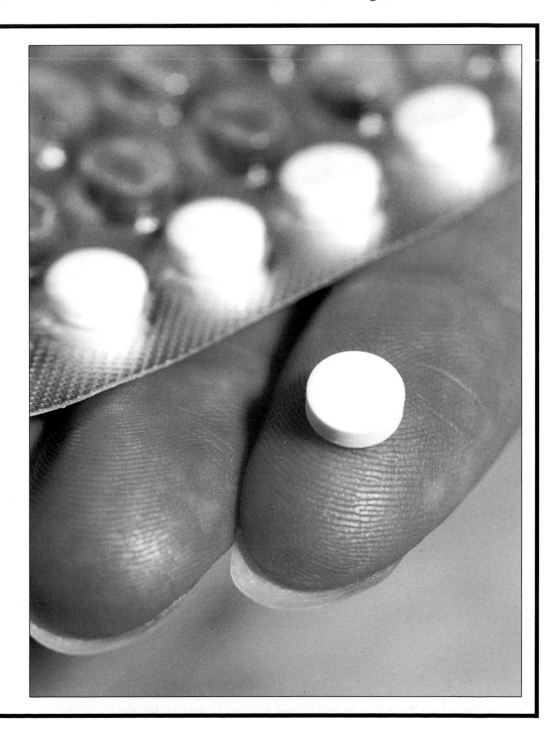

THE FAILING HEART

If your radio or stereo fails, it stops working. If your heart fails, it can go on beating for months or years. But it cannot keep up with the demands of the body and you will start to feel ill.

People with heart failure get tired and out of breath more easily than healthy people, and they may get pains in their chest. Gradually it takes less and less exercise to tire them out, until they find they are breathless even when they are sitting in a chair or lying in bed.

There are several reasons why the heart can start to fail. For example, the heart muscle may have been so badly damaged in a heart attack that it never recovers fully. Or high blood pressure may put too much strain on the heart and make it fail.

No heart gives up without a struggle. When the body realizes that the heart isn't coping very well, it makes it beat faster to try to catch up. Unfortunately, this is the worst thing it can do.

In order to beat faster, the muscle of the left ventricle—the part of the heart that pumps blood to the rest of the body—gets bigger. Before long, you can see on an X ray that the heart is too large. This is quite different from when an athlete's heart gets bigger. In the failing heart, the new heart muscle isn't very efficient. Instead of catching up

This woman suffers from chest pain even when she is sitting down. Her heart can no longer meet the demands made on it by her body.

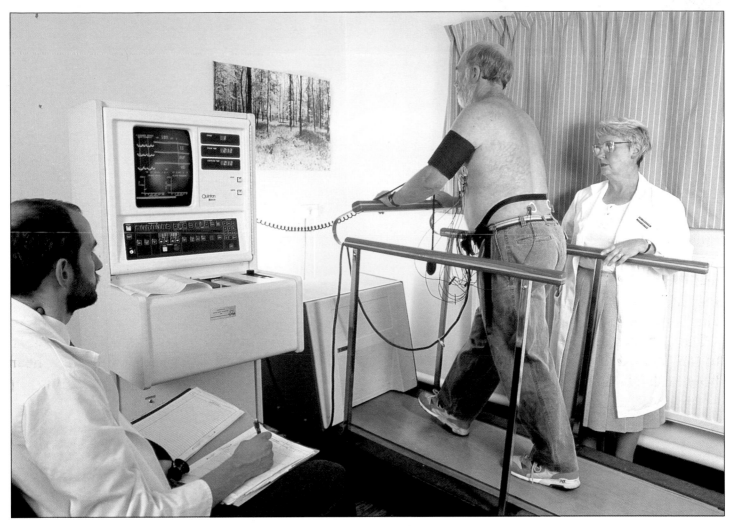

A man is tested to see how well his heart is working while he exercises.

with the demand for blood, the heart falls farther and farther behind.

Doctors use a number of different drugs to try to help the heart. Some drugs make the heart work harder. In the short term, this will help it meet the body's demands. But it puts the heart under even more strain and eventually this may prove too much.

Other drugs make the blood vessels relax so that blood pressure falls. This takes some of the strain off the heart and gives it more time to relax between beats. So it beats more efficiently instead of more quickly.

Recent research suggests that this is a more sensible approach. Although it is not a complete cure, people with heart failure do seem to live longer when they take these drugs.

ON THE TREADMILL

The best way of testing the heart is to put you on a treadmill. Wires stuck to the chest measure how fast the heart is beating and look at the pattern of the heartbeat (EKG). A mask over your face measures how much oxygen you are using while you are on the treadmill.

The speed of the treadmill gradually increases until you are walking quickly or running. How long can you keep going? This is an important measure of how well your heart is working. Your heart rate and the amount of oxygen you use also tell the doctor a lot about the fitness of your heart and whether you need treatment.

STRAIGHT FROM THE HEART

The heart has always held a special place in our society. It is a symbol of love and for centuries it was thought to hold our soul.

As we have seen, however, the heart is just a muscular pump that beats according to instructions from hormones and nerves. There is nothing romantic about it!

When the heart stops, every other part of the body dies. But even when the heart is still beating —and the person is therefore alive—other vital parts of the body may be dead.

If the brain is dead, all life as we know it ends. Someone who is brain-dead cannot think, reason, or understand. He or she cannot feel pain, happiness, hope, or even fear. His or her body becomes an empty shell.

Doctors have devised a number of tests to find out if someone is brain-dead, even though the person's heart is still beating. The tests have been very carefully worked out so that no mistakes are made. People who are brain-dead can be kept "alive" for months or even years by being connected to life-support machines. Their hearts must be able to beat without help. But machines can breathe for them, feed them, and clean their blood.

What sort of life is this? Would you want to be kept alive by machines if your brain was dead?

Due to modern science the heart has lost its sacred place in the body. It does provide the pulse of life, but it is the brain that makes us who we are, and most of us would place a higher value on our minds than our hearts.

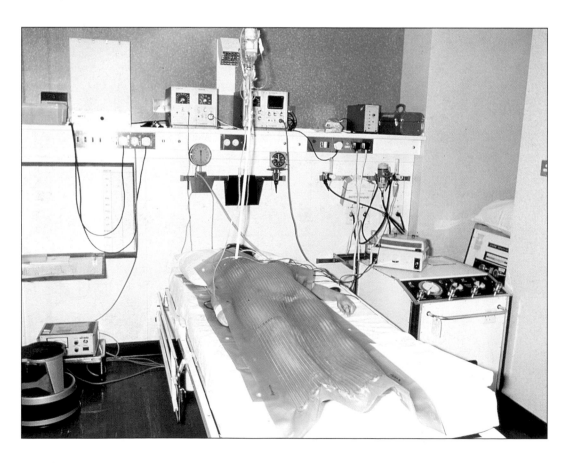

LEFT This patient is being kept alive by machines, but her brain has already died. Her other organs have not been damaged so they may be used in transplant operations to save other people's lives. However, the doctors need her relatives' consent in order to switch off the machine and use her organs in this way.

RIGHT It's a sobering thought; according to current statistics, almost half of the people in this crowd will eventually die of heart disease and circulatory problems.

GLOSSARY

adrenaline—hormone that affects the action of the heart.

AIDS—Acquired Immune Deficiency Syndrome —incurable disease of the immune system, caused by a virus passed on in body fluids, such as blood or semen, that makes the body unable to fight infection.

antibody—protein that can recognize invading organisms as alien and make the body attack them.

aorta—main artery that leaves the heart and branches out to all other parts of the body.

artery—blood vessel that carries blood away from the heart. Nearly all arteries contain oxygenated blood.

atrium—upper part of the heart; every heart normally has two.

biofeedback—relaxation technique used to slow pulse or lower blood pressure.

coronary artery—artery that supplies the heart muscle with blood to give it oxygen and nutrients. The term is also used as slang for a heart attack, since it is a block in one or more coronary arteries that leads to a heart attack.

EKG—the pattern of electrical activity that can be recorded from the heart.

electrode—metal disk used to pick up electrical activity.

embryo—term used to describe a baby in the womb between two and eight weeks after conception.

fetus—term used to describe a baby in the womb from the eighth week after conception until birth.

hemoglobin—pigment in red blood cells that carries oxygen around the body and gives blood its red color.

hepatitis—inflammation of the liver, frequently caused by viral infection.

nerve—hairlike structure that carries messages as electrical signals from the brain to other parts of the body.

nutrient—nourishing part of food that cells need to work normally.

oxygen—vital gas in the air that supports life.

palpitation—rapid, irregular heartbeat.

paralysis—loss of movement or function of part or all of the body due to nerve damage.

pulse—movement of blood in time with the heartbeat that can be felt through the skin.

stroke—block in blood supply to the brain, leading to nerve damage and often paralysis.

vein—blood vessel that carries blood back to the heart. Nearly all veins contain deoxygenated blood.

ventricle—lower part of the heart; a normal heart has two.

BOOKS TO READ

The Circulatory System. Regina Avraham. New York: Chelsea House, 1989.

Eat Well. (Staying Healthy) Miriam Moss. New York: Crestwood House, 1993.

Everything You Need to Know about Smoking. Elizabeth Keyishian. New York: The Rosen Group, 1989.

Exercise. Don Nardo. New York: Chelsea House, 1992.

The Heart and Blood. Revised Edition. Steve Parker. New York: Franklin Watts, 1991.

Heart and Circulatory System Projects for the Young Scientist. Robert E. Dunbar. New York: Franklin Watts, 1989.

Keep Fit. (Staying Healthy) Miriam Moss. New York: Crestwood House, 1993.

The Lungs and Breathing. Revised Edition. Steve Parker. New York: Franklin Watts, 1989.

Medical Technology. Jenny Bryan. New York: Franklin Watts, 1991.

Smoking. Sherry Sonnett. Revised edition by Lorna Greenberg. New York: Franklin Watts, 1989.

Your Heart and Blood. Leslie J. LeMaster. Chicago: Childrens Press, 1984.

ACKNOWLEDGMENTS

Allsport 20 (top), 21 (Simon Bruty); Chapel Studios 10; Colorsport 20 (bottom); Eye Ubiquitos 26 (Roger Chester); Impact 7 (bottom), Christopher Cormack); Life Science Images cover background, 31; Science Photo Library 6 (Petit Format/Nestle), 7 (top, James Stevenson), 11 (Will & Deni McIntyre), 12,13 (top, Dr. Barry Richards), 14 (Blair Seitz), 16 (NIBSC), 19a (top, Phillipe Plailly, bottom, Jerry Mason), 18 (Simon Fraser), 19 (Jerry Mason), 17 (Chris Priest), 32 (CNRI), 33, 34 (Adam Hart-Davis), 36 (Hattie Young), 37 (Rosal), 38, 40 (Dr. Jeremy Burgess), 41 (Andrew McClenaghan), 42 (Chris Priest & Mark Clarke), 43 (Simon Fraser/Coronary Care Unit/Hexham General Hospital), 44 (Biophoto Associates), 45 (Alain le Garsmeur); Ronald Sheridan, Ancient Art & Architecture Collection 4; Tony Stone 23; Topham 8, 13 (bottom), 24, 28; WPL 22, 28, 30; Zefa cover and title page (Al Francekevich), 5 (Tom Casalini), 35, 45. Artwork: Malcolm S. Walker.

INDEX